I Love to Finger Paint!

Jennifer Lipsey

LARK BOOKS

A Division of Sterling Publishing Co., Inc.
New York

My Very Favorite Art Book

This book is dedicated
to my nephews
Cameron, Cole,
and Trenton.

Editor
JOE RHATIGAN

Creative Director
CELIA NARANJO

Art Production Assistant
BRADLEY NORRIS

Assistant Editor
CARLIE RAMER

Editorial Assistance
DELORES GOSNELL

Library of Congress Cataloging-in-Publication Data

Lipsey, Jennifer.
  My very favorite art book : i love to finger paint / Jennifer Lipsey.—
1st ed.
    p. cm.
  Includes index.
   ISBN 1-57990-771-7 (hardcover)
 1. Finger painting—Juvenile literature. I. Title. II. Title: I love to
finger paint.
ND2490.L57 2006
751.4'9—dc22

                                2005034821

10 9 8 7 6 5 4 3 2 1

First Edition

Published by Lark Books, A Division of
Sterling Publishing Co., Inc.
387 Park Avenue South, New York, N.Y. 10016

Distributed in Canada by Sterling Publishing,
c/o Canadian Manda Group, 165 Dufferin Street
Toronto, Ontario, Canada M6K 3H6

Distributed in the United Kingdom by GMC Distribution Services,
Castle Place, 166 High Street, Lewes, East Sussex, England BN7 1XU

Distributed in Australia by Capricorn Link (Australia) Pty Ltd.,
P.O. Box 704, Windsor, NSW 2756 Australia

The written instructions, photographs, designs, patterns, and projects in
this volume are intended for the personal use of the reader and may be
reproduced for that purpose only. Any other use, especially commercial use,
is forbidden under law without written permission of the copyright holder.

Every effort has been made to ensure that all the information in this book
is accurate. However, due to differing conditions, tools, and individual skills,
the publisher cannot be responsible for any injuries, losses, and other
damages that may result from the use of the information in this book.

If you have questions or comments about this book, please contact:
Lark Books
67 Broadway
Asheville, NC 28801
(828) 253-0467

Manufactured in China

ISBN 13: 978-1-57990-771-6
ISBN 10: 1-57990-771-7

For information about custom editions, special sales, and premium and corporate purchases, please
contact Sterling Special Sales Department at 800-805-5489 or specialsales@sterlingpub.com.

Contents

Finger Paint is Fun!

Anyone can finger paint!

All you need are fingers, paint, and paper. When you finger paint, your fingers and hands become the paintbrushes.

This book will show you great ways to use your fingers, hands, and even feet to make awesome art.

Before You Start

- Always ask permission.
- Cover your work area with newspaper, plastic, or an old sheet.
- Put on painting clothes or an apron.
- Keep a bucket of warm, soapy water nearby so you can wash your hands.

Supplies

Paint

Any of these paints will work:
- Tempera paint
- Poster paint
- Acrylic paint
- Homemade paint (see page 46)

Palette

A palette is the thing that holds your paint. It's easier to mix colors if you use one. A palette doesn't have to be fancy. You can try one of these:
- Foam or paper plate
- Egg carton
- Ice tray
- Waxed paper
- Freezer paper

Paper

You don't need special paper to finger paint. For slippery paper, try these:
- Freezer paper
- Magazine pages
- Waxed paper
- Foam plates

Other papers you can use:
- Newspaper
- Construction paper
- Copy paper
- Wrapping paper

Other Stuff

To do some of the projects in this book you will need to have these supplies handy:
- Sponges
- Markers
- Paper towels
- Scissors
- Paintbrushes
- Water cups

Keep a wet paper towel nearby every time you're fingerpainting to clean your hands between color changes. Also, remember to wait until your painting is dry before drawing on it. And if you want your painting to dry faster, have an adult blow it with a hair dryer.

How to Finger Paint

1. Touch the paint on your palette.

2. Use your finger as a paintbrush on the paper. It's as easy as that!

Finger Printing

Make a Fingerprint

1. Press your finger on a paint pad (see below) or paint your finger with a brush.
2. Press your finger down onto your paper. Let the paint dry before you draw on it.
3. Before changing colors, clean your fingers on a wet paper towel.

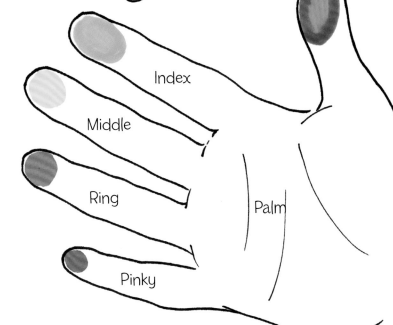

Thumb

Index

Middle

Ring

Palm

Pinky

Make a Two-Color Fingerprint

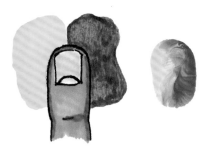

1. Put two colors close together on your paint pad or palette. Press a finger on both colors at the same time. Now print.

Make a Paint Pad

1. Fold a wet paper towel and put it on a plate.
2. Brush paint onto it.
3. If the pad starts to dry out, spray it with some water. Add more paint as you need it.

Hand Printing

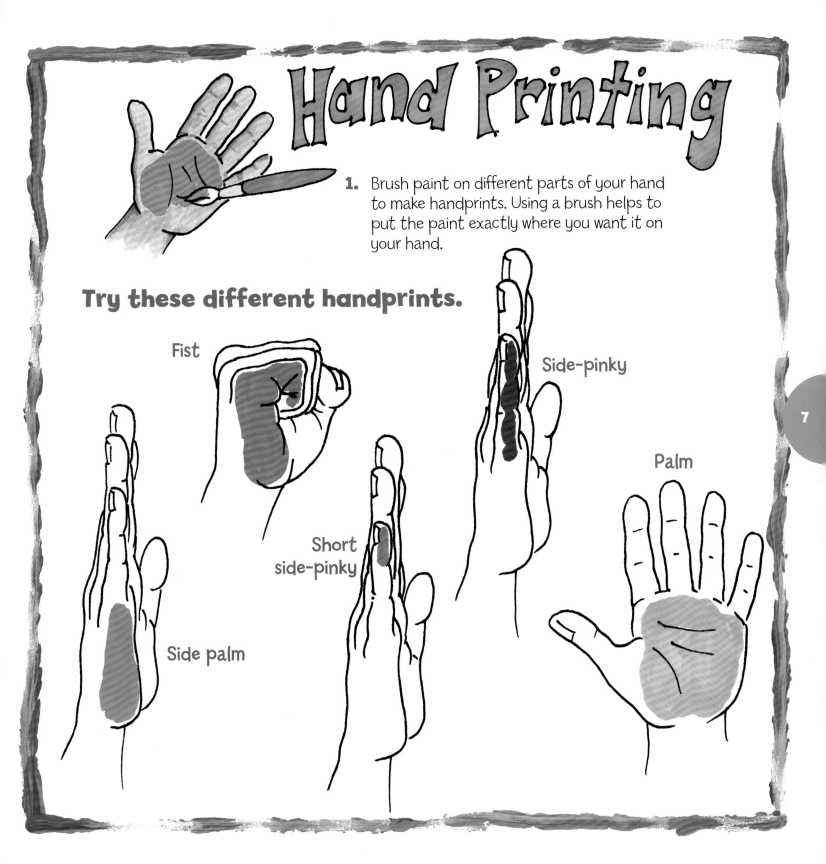

1. Brush paint on different parts of your hand to make handprints. Using a brush helps to put the paint exactly where you want it on your hand.

Try these different handprints.

Fist

Side-pinky

Palm

Short side-pinky

Side palm

Trees

1. Finger paint a big letter Y for the tree trunk.

2. Paint the letter V on the end of each branch. This will make more branches. Let it dry.

3. Use fingerprints to make a bunch of leaves. Use two fingers at the same time, if you want.

Try This!

Paint more than one tree in the same picture.

OR

To make a really big tree, keep adding more Vs to the end of each branch.

Supplies
- Paint
- Paper
- Palette
- Wet paper towel
- Water cup

Spring

Use your pinky to print flowers in your tree.

Summer

Use your ring finger to print apples.

How about a butterfly?

Fall

Print some leaves on the ground.

Winter

Paint a sky first. Let it dry. Paint a tree, and then add snow on top of the branches and on the ground.

Under the Sea

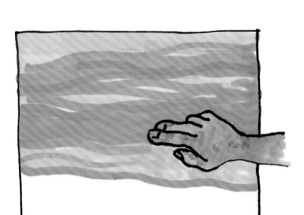

1. Use different colors of blue and green to finger paint water. Leave space for sand. Let it dry.

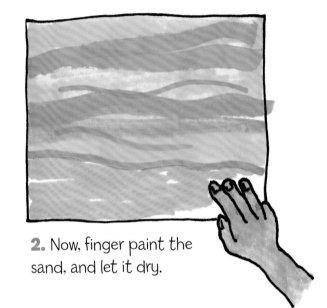

2. Now, finger paint the sand, and let it dry.

3. Finger paint different sea creatures and sea plants.

Once your painting is dry, use a small paintbrush or marker to add details such as eyes, stripes, and dots.

Supplies

- Paint
- Paper
- Palette
- Wet paper towel
- Water cup
- Small paintbrush or marker

Can you think of other sea creatures? How about a handprint fish?

Paint a shell.

Try a starfish. Draw a star first, and then finger paint over it.

Printed Patterns

A pattern is something that repeats itself over and over. You can create patterns with colors, shapes, or both.

Color pattern

O□△O□△O□△

Shape pattern

1. Lightly draw a big shape with a pencil.

2. Finger print a color pattern following the pencil line.

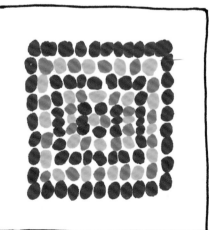

3. Keep printing until the whole shape is filled.

What other patterns can you think of?

Supplies
- Pencil
- Paper
- Paint
- Palette
- Wet paper towel
- Water cup

Print a hat.
Add details
with markers
if you want.

Try a striped
pattern.

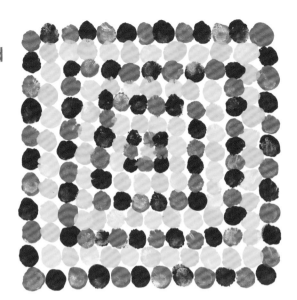

13

Use a zigzag
pattern for a
Christmas tree.
Finger print
ornaments
after it dries.

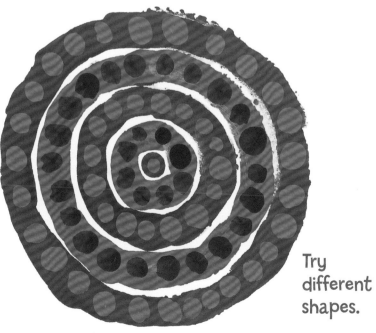

Try
different
shapes.

Scrape & Scratch

1. Finger paint the whole paper.

2. While your painting is still wet, use one of the tools to gently scrape or scratch a picture into the paint.

Try This!

1. Cut small pieces from the side of a piece of cardboard. Ask an adult for help.

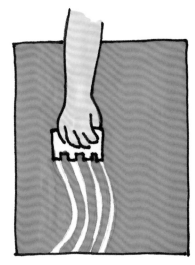

2. Pull and scrape over the wet painting. Awesome!

Supplies

- Paint
- Paper
- Palette
- Wet paper towel
- Water cup
- Scratching tools: your fingernails, paintbrush handle, plastic forks and spoons, cardboard

Try painting your paper and letting it dry. Then, paint it again with a different color. While it's still wet, scratch a drawing so the first color shows through.

Try a tree!

How about a pet portrait?

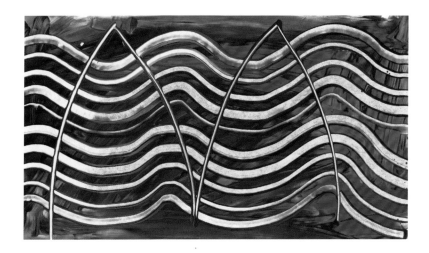

Finger Food

What do you like to eat? Try finger painting something tasty!

Finger paint a carrot. When the carrot is dry, draw lines on it.

Are you in the mood for grapes? Finger paint some.

Yum, finger printed peanuts. Draw small lines on the peanuts after they dry.

Who wants corn on the cob?

Supplies

- Paint
- Paper
- Palette
- Wet paper towel
- Water cup
- Markers

Make some finger painted celery. Use fingerprints to make leaves.

Two overlapping fingerprints make a strawberry. After the strawberries dry, use a thin black marker to make small lines on them.

Try scratching lines in the celery stalk with a fingernail while the paint is still wet.

Finger paint a sandwich as big as you like!

Slithery Scales

Overlapping fingerprints make
cool scales for slithery creatures.

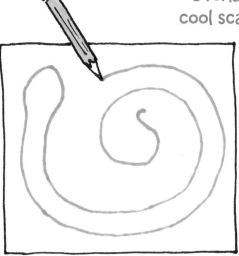

1. Use a pencil to lightly draw a simple creature that has scales.

2. Start at the end of the body and finger print a row of scales. Change colors if you want to. Finger print another row that overlaps the first row.

3. Keep printing rows of overlapping scales until you fill up the body.

Finger paint the parts that don't have scales such as fins, wings, and heads.

If it helps, turn your paper while you print.

Can you think of
other scaled
creatures?
A sea monster?
A dragon?

Add a rattle.

Landscapes

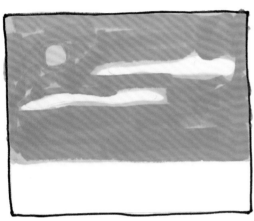

1. Finger paint a sky. Do you want clouds, a sun, a moon? When you're done, let it dry.

2. Now, finger paint the land. Do you want the land to be flat or hilly? Let it dry.

3. Finger paint trees, people, buildings, or anything you want.

Supplies

• Paint
• Paper
• Palette
• Wet paper towel
• Water cup
• Markers

Let the cactus dry before adding pricklies.

Mix red, orange, and yellow for a sunset. Finger print some coconuts.

Spacescape

1. Use black paper or paint a piece of paper black. Use an old toothbrush to spatter white paint to make stars.

2. Paint part of a planet or moon so that it looks close up. Add curved lines of a darker color to make craters.

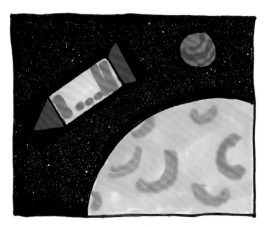

Use markers or a small paintbrush to add details.

3. Add more planets or moons. How about a rocket?

Supplies

- Paint
- Paper
- Palette
- Old toothbrush
- Wet paper towel
- Water cup
- Markers or small paintbrush

What else can you finger
paint in your spacescape?

A shooting star?
An alien?
A spaceship?
A space station?
A satellite?
The sun?

Add details to your rocket using fingerprints
and lines.

Flowers

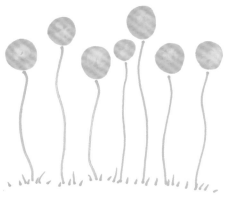

Use your ring finger to make flowers. Finger paint the stems.

Make ring fingerprints. Pinky print a different color on top. Add stems and grass when it dries.

Finger paint cattails. Brush the stems.

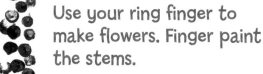

Paint or draw long lines. Use short side-pinky prints to make fern leaves.

Short side-pinky print petals. Ring finger print leaves. Paint the stems with a brush.

Supplies

- Paint
- Paper
- Palette
- Wet paper towel
- Water cup
- Skinny paintbrush
- Markers
- Damp sponge (optional)

Print two-color fingerprints for these leaves. (See page 6.)

Use a marker for small details.

To make your flowers look fuzzy, wet your paper with a sponge before you paint.

Paint a red and purple blob. Scratch lines in the blob with your fingernail to make a rose.

Sponge Fingers

1. Have an adult cut a slightly damp sponge into finger-sized strips.

2. Fold a sponge strip in half. Put a small rubber band around it.

3. Put the sponge on the tip of your finger. Dip your finger into some paint and see what you can do!

Try This!

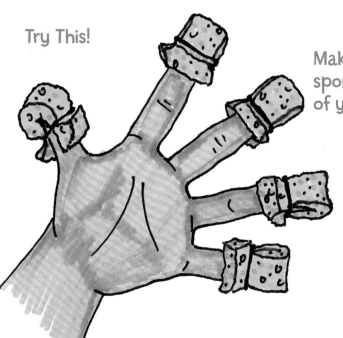

Make a finger sponge for each of your fingers.

Try different colors on each finger sponge.

Supplies

- Sponge
- Scissors
- Rubber bands
- Paint
- Paper
- Palette
- Water cup
- Markers

Make a plaid design.

1. Put sponge fingers on your three middle fingers.

2. Dip them into three different colors.

3. Hold your sponge fingers together while you paint stripes.

4. Turn your paper and make stripes going the other way.

Sponge flowers!

How about spongebots?

Use your sponge fingers to fill the whole paper with swirls, blobs, prints, and lines.

Paint & Print

Make a one-of-a-kind copy of your painting. This is called a monoprint.

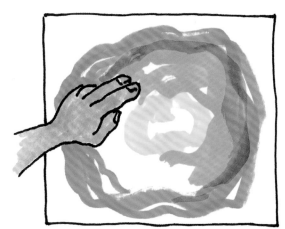

1. Finger paint a picture or a design on paper.

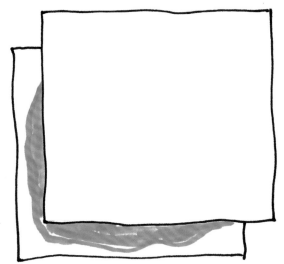

2. While your painting is still wet, lay a blank piece of paper on top of it. Press them together.

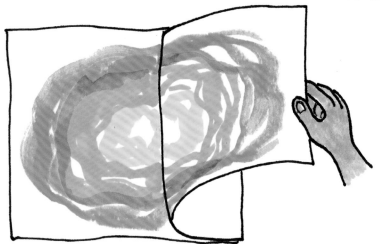

3. Now, peel the layers apart. You have a print of your own painting.

Supplies
- Paint
- Paper
- Palette
- Wet paper towel
- Water cup

Here is the painting ...   and here is the print!

Painting

Print

Painting   Print

Creep & Crawl

Ant

1. Make three ring finger fingerprints in a row.

2. After they are dry, add legs and antennae with a black marker.

Ant from Above

1. Draw legs on both sides.

Inchworm

1. Finger paint two lines with a space in between.

2. Use an upside-down U to connect the lines.

Centipede

1. Add more fingerprints and legs to make a centipede.

Ladybug

1. Make a red middle fingerprint.

2. Overlap a black ring fingerprint.

3. Use your pinky finger to make spots. Let it dry.

4. Use a marker to draw legs, antennae, and wings.

Spider

1. Make a middle fingerprint.

2. Make a sideways index fingerprint that overlaps a little.

3. Use a marker to make legs and a mouth.

Supplies

- Paint
- Paper
- Palette
- Wet paper towel
- Water cup
- Markers

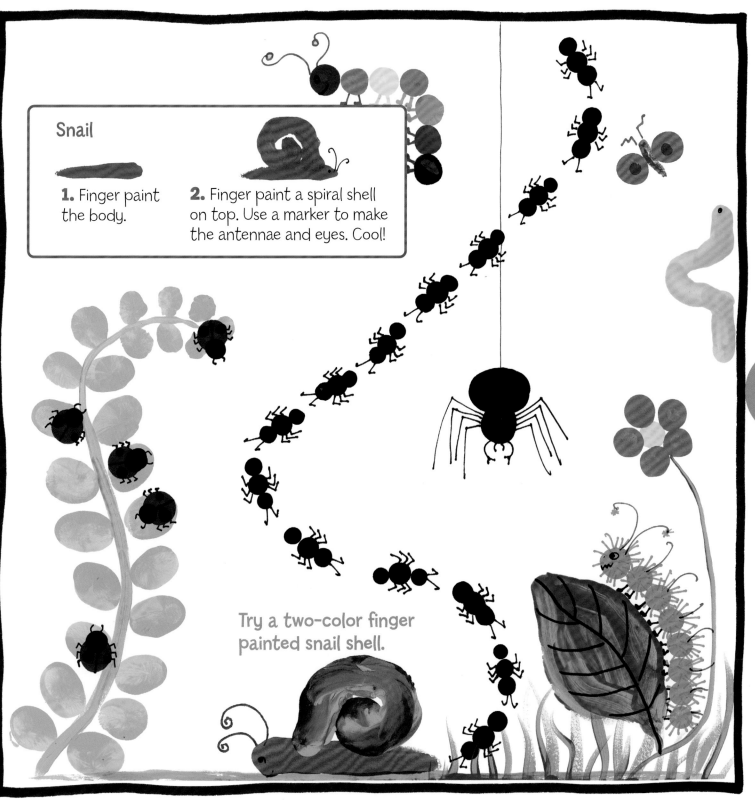

Snail

1. Finger paint the body.

2. Finger paint a spiral shell on top. Use a marker to make the antennae and eyes. Cool!

Try a two-color finger painted snail shell.

Fly & Flutter

Small Butterfly

1. Make a print with the small side of your pinky.

2. Use your ring finger to make wings.

Bumble Bee

1. Make a yellow thumbprint. Use your ring finger to make a print on top of the thumbprint.

2. Use the small side of your pinky to print stripes. Draw wings.

3. Draw legs, stingers, and antennae.

Big Butterfly

1. Make a print with your pinky.

2. Make thumbprints for the wings.

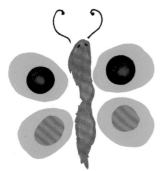

3. Decorate the wings with smaller fingerprints. Draw the antennae.

Dragonfly

1. Make a print for the body with the side of your pinky. Ring finger print the head.

2. Finger paint the wings. Draw the antennae.

House Fly

1. Make a ring fingerprint.

2. Draw wings and legs with a marker.

33

Foot Prints

Before you start, spread out plenty of newspaper or an old sheet. Help from a friend makes this project more fun and easier to do.

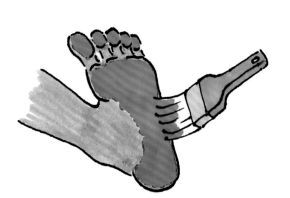

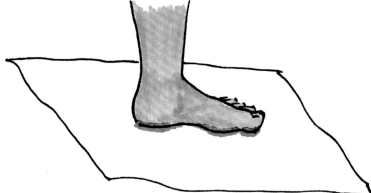

1. Use a large paintbrush to paint the bottom of your foot.

2. Press your foot onto a big piece of paper. Have your friend hold the paper down as you take your foot off it. Wash your foot in a bucket of soapy water.

Try This!

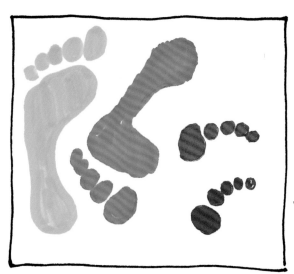

Try making patterns and designs using footprints.

Try printing just your toes!

Supplies
- Newspapers or old bed sheet
- Large paintbrush
- Paint
- Palette
- Big sheets of paper
- Paper towels
- Water cup

Try making overlapping footprints.

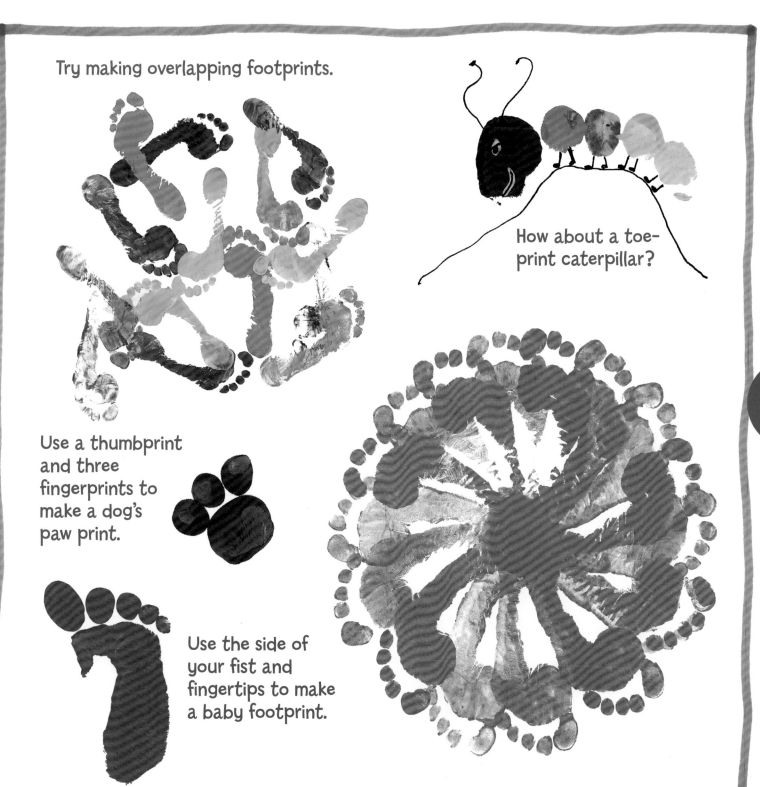

How about a toe-print caterpillar?

Use a thumbprint and three fingerprints to make a dog's paw print.

Use the side of your fist and fingertips to make a baby footprint.

Funny Faces

Use your palms and fingers to make funny faces!

1. Paint your palm with the paintbrush.

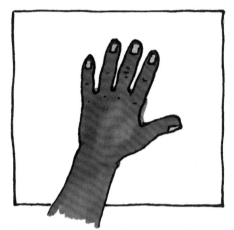

2. Press your palm against the paper. Use your other hand to help push down the center of your palm.

3. Thumb print the ears. Finger print some hair.

4. Make the face look as silly as you want.

Make eyes, eyebrows, a nose, a mouth, earrings, and anything else you can think of.

Supplies

- Paint
- Paintbrush
- Paper
- Palette
- Wet paper towel
- Water cup
- Markers

Can you guess which fingers were
used to decorate these faces?

"I've got my eye on you!"

Finger paint the monster
mouth black. After it dries,
print some teeth.

After your picture is
dry, add more details
with markers.

Try adding a body!

How about sunglasses?

Palm Print Pets

Use your palm to print your pet's body.
Use other parts of your hand and fingers to print
legs, paws, ears, and tails (see page 9).

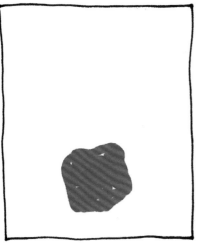

1. Paint your palm with the paintbrush and print it.

2. Paint your palm again and make another print above the first one.

3. Upside-down side palm prints make long ears. Thumbprints make paws. Ring finger-prints make the eyes and a nose. Use a marker to make whiskers when the face is dry.

Supplies

- Paint
- Paper
- Palette
- Paintbrush
- Wet paper towel
- Water cup
- Markers

Fist print ears

Three palm prints make the dog's body and head.

Add details with a marker after your painting is dry.

Long pinky print a tail.

Three palm prints make the cat's body.

Long finger-prints make the ears and legs.

One palm print makes the turtle's body.

Printed People

You can use fingerprints and handprints (see page 7) to create wild and wacky people!

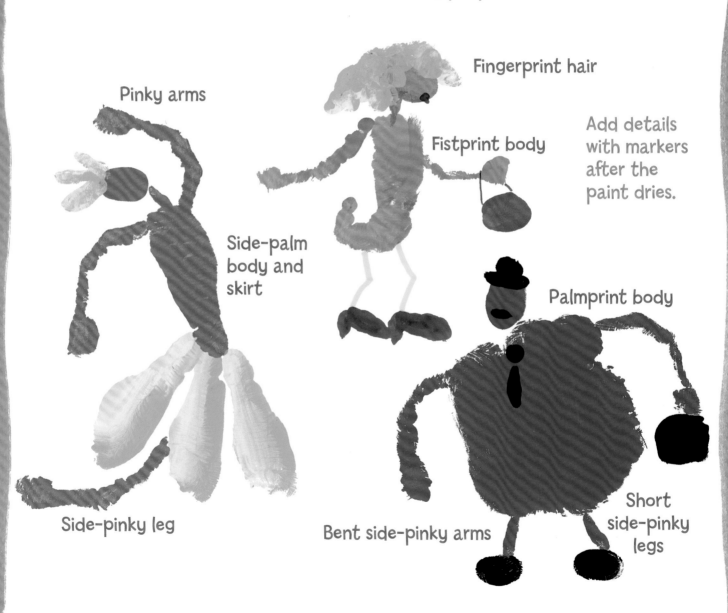

Pinky arms

Fingerprint hair

Fistprint body

Add details with markers after the paint dries.

Side-palm body and skirt

Palmprint body

Side-pinky leg

Bent side-pinky arms

Short side-pinky legs

Short side-pinky hair

Ring finger arms and legs

Make up your own silly people!

Fist arms

Side-palm legs

Try adding faces!

41

Recycled Art

Now that you've got tons of finger painted masterpieces around the house, you might have a few you're tired of. Good! Here's how to make your old art into a new masterpiece.

1. Finger paint a background, and let it dry.

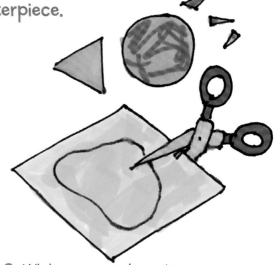

2. While your painting dries, use a pencil to draw simple shapes on your old paintings. Cut out the shapes.

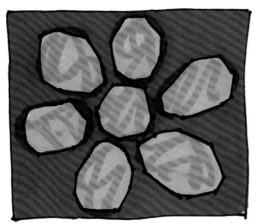

3. Glue your cut-out shapes to the new finger-painted background to make a scene or design. Wow!

Supplies

- Paint
- Paper
- Palette
- Wet paper towel
- Water cup
- Paintings to cut out
- Pencil
- Scissors
- Glue

Try a handscape!

How about a flower?

Paint & Cut

1. Finger paint a few pieces of paper in different colors. Try painting two colors on one sheet. Let them dry.

2. Cut the painted paper into long strips.

3. Cut the strips into squares. Make a separate pile for each color.

4. Draw a large shape such as a sun, flower, or a fish on the black paper.

5. Put a small dot of glue on your pencil line. Stick a colored square to the line. Outline the whole shape with squares. Fill in the shape with squares.

6. Fill in the background using a different color.

Supplies
- Paint
- Thick paper
- Palette
- Wet paper towel
- Water cup
- Scissors
- Pencil
- Black paper
- Glue

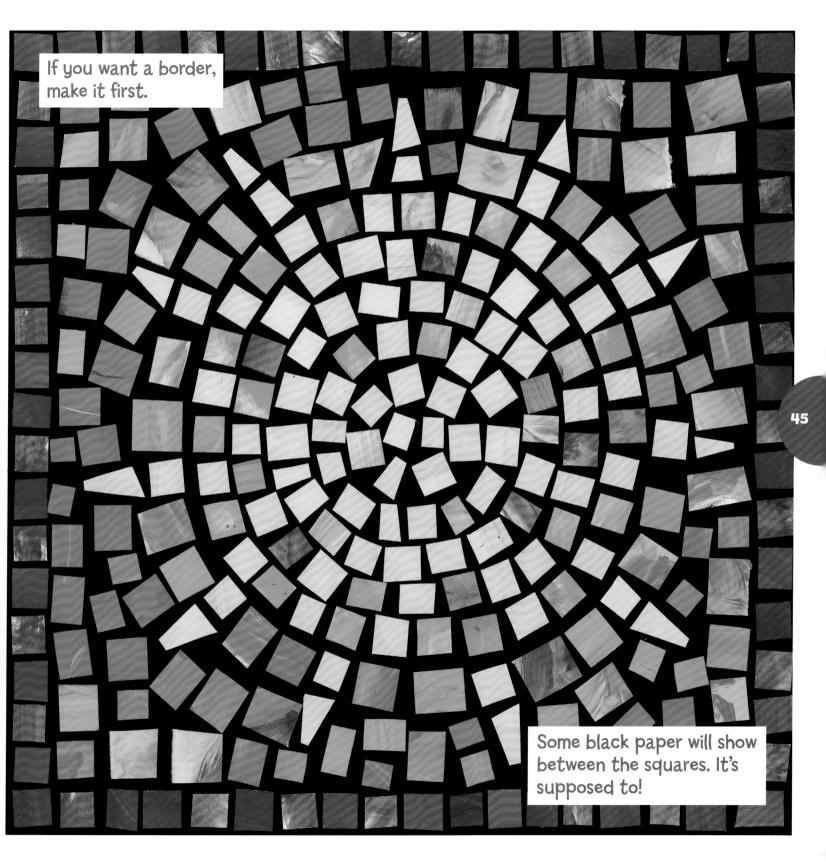

If you want a border, make it first.

45

Some black paper will show between the squares. It's supposed to!

More Finger Fun!

Here are some easy recipes to follow for making your own finger paints. Try them all!

Shaving Cream Paint

1. Spray shaving cream onto a big piece of freezer paper, waxed paper, or a table that is not made of wood.

2. Sprinkle a few drops of tempera paint into the shaving cream.

3. Watch the colors mix as you finger paint with the shaving cream.

Pudding or Yogurt Paint

1. Freezer paper, waxed paper, or a foam plate are all good to paint on for this project. They make licking up easy!

2. Put vanilla pudding or yogurt into a few small cups.

3. Stir two or three drops of food coloring into each cup.

4. Use your fingers to paint away!

Bathtub Paint

1. In a small bowl, mix together ⅓ of a cup of dish soap or shampoo with a spoonful of cornstarch.

2. Pour the mixture into four sections of an egg carton or an ice cube tray.

3. Mix one or two drops of different colors of food coloring into each section. Go take a bath!

Wash away your painting when you're done.

Flour Paint

1. Put ½ cup of water, ½ cup of flour, and a spoonful of salt in a bowl. Mix together well. If the mixture is too thick, add more water. If the mixture is too thin, add more flour.

2. Pour the mixture into sections of an egg carton, an ice cube tray, or some small cups.

3. Mix a few drops of tempera paint into each section to make different colors.

Now finger paint!

Try a Texture

Mix one of the items from this list with paint to create a new texture:

- Sand
- Sawdust
- Coffee grounds
- Dry oatmeal
- Sugar

- Dry tea
- Flour
- Dirt
- Rice
- Salt

How does the paint feel when you mix it with sand?

Does the paint smell any different when you mix it with coffee?

Be sure to let your painting dry on a flat surface overnight.

Acknowledgments

Thank you to the Great Artist for the ability and opportunity to spread the joy of art to so many young people.

Kids are capable of extraordinary things and need only to be given the chance to express their built-in creativity. Thanks to the parents, grandparents, aunts, uncles, and friends who provide these opportunities by purchasing books such as this one. You make a difference in kids' lives!

I am grateful to the many family members, friends, art-world professionals, booksellers, students, educators, parents, and the folks at Lark Books who have stood behind the **My Very Favorite Art Book** series. Thank you.

Special thanks to my own parents, Denise and Jim, Karen and Steve, and Barb and Glenn who continue to inspire confidence and determination in my work. Your love and support is priceless.

As always, heartfelt thanks to Martin for his never-ending love and encouragement.

Index